Places to Work

by Helen Gregory

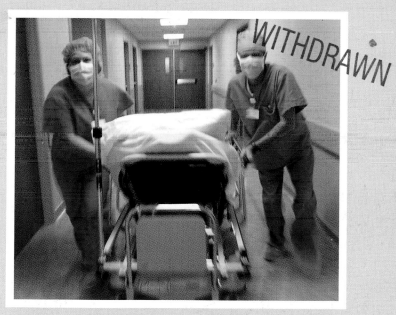

Consultant:
Adria F. Klein, PhD
California State University, San Bernardino

CAPSTONE PRESS
a capstone imprint

Wonder Readers are published by Capstone Press,
1710 Roe Crest Drive, North Mankato, Minnesota 56003.
www.capstonepub.com

Library of Congress Cataloging-in-Publication Data
Gregory, Helen.
  Places to work / Gregory, Helen.
    p. cm.—(Wonder readers)
  Includes index.
  ISBN 978-1-4765-0043-0 (library binding)
  ISBN 978-1-4296-7806-3 (paperback)
  ISBN 978-1-4765-0855-9 (eBook PDF)
  1. Work environment—Juvenile literature. 2. Occupations—Juvenile literature. I. Title. II. Series.
  HD7261.C627 2013
  331.702—dc23   2011023871

Summary: Describes a variety of jobs and places where people work.

Editorial Credits
Maryellen Gregoire, project director; Mary Lindeen, consulting editor; Gene Bentdahl, designer;
Sarah Schuette, editor; Wanda Winch, media researcher; Eric Manske, production specialist

Photo Credits
Photos by Capstone Studio: Karon Dubke except: Shutterstock: Yuri Arcurs, 4

Word Count: **92**   Guided Reading Level: **F**   Early Intervention Level: **9**

Printed in China.
092012   006934LEOS13

Table of Contents

Note to Parents and Teachers

The Wonder Readers Next Steps: Social Studies series supports national social studies standards. These titles use text structures that support early readers, specifically with a close photo/text match and glossary. Each book is perfectly leveled to support the reader at the right reading level, and the topics are of high interest. Early readers will gain success when they are presented with a book that is of interest to them and is written at the appropriate level.

Going to Work

People go to work
in the morning.

Some people work
in offices.

This doctor works
at the hospital.

This **scientist** works
in a lab.

This police officer works at an office.

This dentist works
in a **clinic**.

Working Outside

This garbage collector works in town.

This farmer works
in the fields.

Working with Others

This reporter works
where there is news.

This teacher works
in a classroom.

People at Work

This **security guard** works at the mall.

This firefighter works
at the fire station.

This **lifeguard** works
at a pool.

This **florist** works
at a store.

Where do you work?

Now Try This!

On a sheet of paper, make a list of all of the places people work in this book. Then write down the kind of work you would like to do when you grow up. Finally, name the places where you would do that work.

Glossary

clinic	a building where people go to receive medical care
florist	someone who sells flowers and plants
lifeguard	a person trained to help swimmers
scientist	a person who studies the world around us
security guard	a person who works to keep a place safe from criminals

Internet Sites

FactHound offers a safe, fun way to find Internet sites related to this book. All of the sites on FactHound have been researched by our staff.

Here's all you do:

Visit *www.facthound.com*

Type in this code: 9781476500430

Super-cool stuff!

Check out projects, games and lots more at
www.capstonekids.com

Index